To Philip M.J.
To Gabriel and Clara A.W.

Text by Mary Joslin
Illustrations copyright © 1997 Alison Wisenfeld
This edition copyright © 2014 Lion Hudson

Published by Lion Children's Books
an imprint of
Lion Hudson plc
Wilkinson House, Jordan Hill Road,
Oxford OX2 8DR, England
www.lionhudson.com/lionchildrens

ISBN 978 0 7459 6492 8

First edition 1997
This edition 2014

A catalogue record for this book is available from the British Library

Printed and bound in China, February 2014, LH17

SAINT FRANCIS

THE GOOD MAN OF ASSISI

Mary Joslin

Illustrations by
Alison Wisenfeld

LION
CHILDREN'S

Long ago, in the busy little town of Assisi, a wealthy merchant and his wife had a baby boy. They wanted to give their little son all the good things their money could buy.

The boy was called Francis.
He liked poems
and songs
and parties.
He grew up rich.
He grew up strong.

Francis longed to be a knight.
He wanted to show he was strong,
to win great battles for a powerful lord.
The first time he went to war,
he was taken prisoner.
His friends had to pay
to free him.

The second time he set out, he had a dream. He was told to go home and learn to serve a different lord, the Lord God.

But back home in Assisi, Francis wondered just what to do. His friends said, "You know what makes a good party. You can be lord of our parties."

And so he was. Francis liked to give to others and he spent lots of money on food and drink.

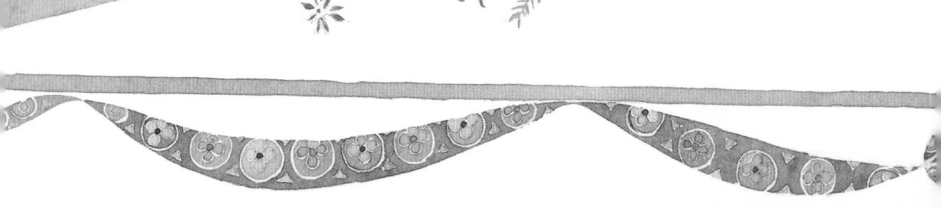

* When everyone was eating and drinking and singing noisy songs, Francis remembered God.

He remembered Jesus, born to show God's goodness to the world.

Francis remembered words of Jesus he had read in the Bible: "Sell what you have and give the money to poor people. And come, follow me."

Francis took off his fine clothes and gave them to the poor.

Jesus said, "Anyone who wants to follow me must give up everything else."

Francis left his home to go about the world telling people of Jesus.

Jesus loved those who were not strong. He healed the sick. So Francis helped people who were ill and was a friend to those who were weak.

Above all, Jesus said,
"Love one another as
I have loved you."

Some people think only
of themselves. Francis
helped others.

Some people find things
to hate about others.
Francis looked for the good
in everyone.

Some people get angry and shout. Francis spoke gently and tried to bring peace.

Some people are sad. Some have no one who loves them. Some have bad things happen to them.

Francis was a friend to them. He showed them that God loved them.

And he gave them hope.

More and more people came to see Francis and hear what he had to say.

Many people changed their lives to live more like Jesus.

Some decided to live like Francis. They were known as friars.

Others stayed at home,
living simply, loving greatly,
and making their world more
gentle and lovely.

Francis believed
everything was
made by God
and was very,
very good.

So he admired the little things. He loved the wriggly worms and would stop to lift them from harm.

He admired the great and wonderful things of the world. He loved the golden sun of daytime and the moon and stars in the night sky.

He wanted the flowers to sing
to God their Maker.

He wanted all the lovely
things of earth and fire,
air and water to love their
Maker...

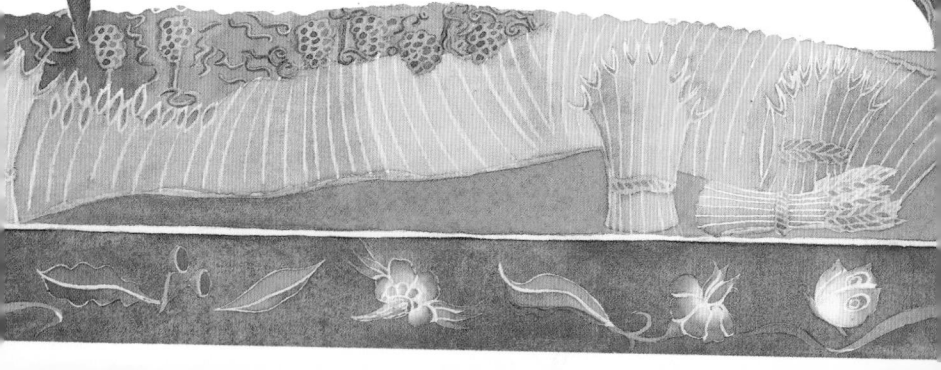

to show their love
by doing the things
for which God had
created them.

All things he called brother or sister, and living things loved him and followed him.

Francis talked to the birds about God their Maker.

He told them always to thank God who gave them clear air to fly in and food to eat.

Then Francis said a prayer for them, and let them fly away, singing God's praises.

In the same way, Francis told all birds, animals, and reptiles to praise God and to love God.

And Francis wanted all people to praise God, and to remember that God, who is rich beyond all dreaming, had come to earth as a poor baby – the baby Jesus.

One December, Francis asked a good man to prepare a stable like the one in Bethlehem so long before, where Jesus had been cradled in a manger.

Men and women saw the stable and remembered Jesus.

In time, Francis grew weak and ill. He remembered that God, who is strong beyond all imagining, had come to earth as Jesus and become weak.

Angry people had put Jesus to death on a cross of wood.

Francis wanted to follow Jesus in every way and, by a miracle, he was given the same wounds that Jesus had on his hands, his feet, and his side.

Francis died poor. He died weak. But he died gladly. He trusted Jesus' promise that death would take him close to God: safe for ever.

Lord, make me a channel of your peace.
Where there is hatred, let me sow love,
Where there is injury, pardon,
Where there is doubt, faith,
Where there is despair, hope,
Where there is darkness, light,
Where there is sadness, joy.
O Divine Master, grant that I may not so much
seek to be consoled as to console, not so much to
be understood as to understand, not so much
to be loved as to love; for it is in giving that we
receive, it is in pardoning that we are pardoned,
it is in dying that we awake to eternal life.

A prayer for those who want to follow Jesus as Francis did